Praises for

Covered in
CHOCOLATE

Engaging. Creative. Innovative. *Covered in Chocolate* won't collect dust on a shelf. This book is a wonderful compilation of hands-on educational activities that engage children…making learning pure joy.

—Karen Perkins
Curriculum Director, Danville, Indiana

Covered in Chocolate is every educator's wish and every child's dream! This book will be cherished among students and teachers alike.

—Erin Bronson
Teacher, Alexandria, Virginia

Covered in Chocolate is enticing to home-school families, classroom educators, parents, and grandparents. Anyone who desires to be involved in their child's education or to share meaningful activities together should own a copy. Our children ultimately benefit!

—Kristen Conley
Home-school Parent, Wheaton, Illinois

Covered in CHOCOLATE

Jim & Helen —
Enjoy getting
covered in chocolate
with your
grandchildren!

Covered in CHOCOLATE

child-centered recipes, chocolate-inspired curriculum

a deliciously fun cookbook by

Lizzie Lou

TATE PUBLISHING & *Enterprises*

Published by Tate Publishing & Enterprises, LLC
127 E. Trade Center Terrace | Mustang, Oklahoma 73064 USA
1.888.361.9473 | www.tatepublishing.com

Tate Publishing is committed to excellence in the publishing industry. The company reflects the philosophy established by the founders, based on Psalm 68:11,
"The Lord gave the word and great was the company of those who published it."

Book design copyright © 2009 by Tate Publishing, LLC. All rights reserved.
Cover and interior design by Elizabeth A. Mason
Illustrations by Kathy Hoyt

Published in the United States of America

ISBN: 978-1-60799-440-4
1. Juvenile Nonfiction: Cooking & Food
2. Juvenile Nonfiction: Social Issues: Values & Virtues
09.05.19

DEDICATION

This cookbook is dedicated to my loving parents, Randall and Helen Germann.

Winter evenings…
homemade hot puddings.

Spring mornings…
crepes with warm maple syrup.

Summer afternoons…
hand-dipped milkshakes.

Fall weekends…
cinnamon monkey bread.

Dear Mom and Dad,

Thank you for taking time to teach me to adore being creative in the kitchen. Your warm hospitality and the time you spend in thoughtful preparation is a wonderful gift you continue to give others. You were (and still are!) a great team. I feel incredibly blessed to be your daughter. Thank you for making "home" a wonderful place to be!

I love you,
Lizzie Lou

*Note to reader: the letters B and E are being used to help children see which recipes are easy and which are harder.

B = Beginner

E = Expert

Table of CONTENTS

Introduction   19

Sammy's Safety Tips   21

Consulate of Cake County

(B) Popcorn Cake   26

(E) Myrtle Turtle Cupcakes   28

(E) Toppin' It Off Cupcakes!   30

(E) German Chocolate Pound Cake   32

(E) Choc-O-Chip Bundt Cake   34

(E) Cocoa Cakes   36

KING OF THE COOKIE KINGDOM

(B) Munchin' Malts   42

(B) Nuttylicious Bars   44

(B) Party in a Pan!   46

(E) P-Nut Cookies   48

(E) "Never-too-late for   50
      choc-o-late" Bars

(E) Oat Chocochippers   52

(E) Colossal Cake Cookies   54

Guru of Glacial Goodies

(B) Chocoalamondo Shake 60

(B) Nanachocolicious Pops 62

(B) Hands Off My Malt! 64

(B) Wafflelicious Ice Cream Towers 66

(B) Homemade Ice Cream Sandwiches 68

(B) NanaSplit Shake 70

(B) Chocolate-covered Strawberry 72
    Shake-up

Duchess of Desirable Desserts

(B) Chocolate Soup 78

(B) Red Carpet Truffles 80

(B) Hazelnut S'mores 84

(B) More S'mores Please! 86

(B) Won't Budge For Fudge! 88

(B) Peanut Butter Whirlwind Fudge 90

(E) Luscious…Layer Upon Layer! 92

(E) Dog-Gone-It…these are good! 94
    Bones for Man's Best Friend

THE BONBON BARON

(B) "Nutty" about Chocolate!   100

(B) An Edible Turtle?   102

(B) Peanut Candy   104

(B) Kaboodle Moodles   106

(B) Joys   108

How is chocolate made, anyway?   111

Appetite for Learning   115

Stuff You May Want to Know!

Measurement Key   128

Glossary   129

Meet Patty!

Perfect and Precise

Patty has a passion for fashion—always looking her best!

She is precise and particular when it comes to styling her hair, checking her homework, and cooking in the kitchen.

Patty is perfect in every way!

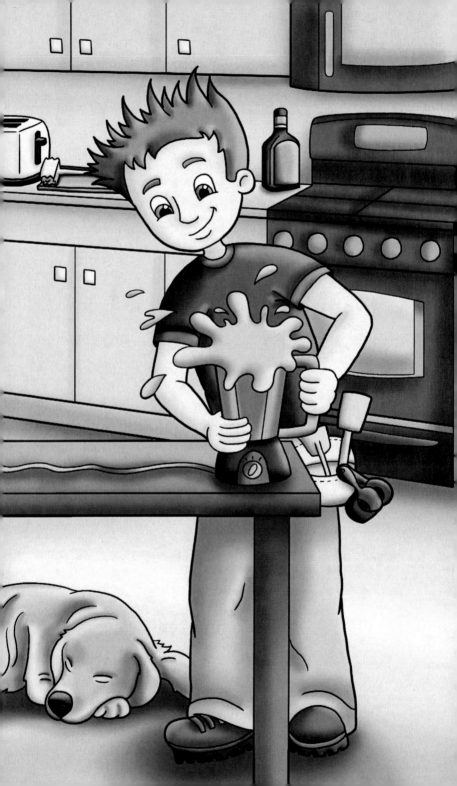

Meet Sammy!

SAFETY FIRST!

Sammy is calculated, concise, and considers all possibilities when in the kitchen.

Equipped with necessary safety gear, Sammy takes careful precaution while cooking.

Sammy's motto is "Safety First!"

Meet Maddy!
CAREFREE AND SPUNKY

Maddy loves life!

She makes a disaster of any kitchen, but the craziness doesn't phase her.

Maddy smiles in the midst of the mess!

INTRODUCTION

Measuring, mixing, and making a mess...
It's what we do best!

We have looked forward to meeting you! The three of us are excited to make a mess with you in the kitchen. We couldn't be more different from one another—the way we look, our personalities—but we do have three things in common.

1. We are "Chocoholics."
2. We have a blast together.
3. We are eager for you to join us!

The first portion of *Covered in Chocolate* is a collection of our very favorite recipes. Chocolate is our superstar ingredient, and it oozes through every recipe in this book. We are certain you will love making (and eating!) these treats. The second portion of the book allows you to peek inside a chocolate factory and see how chocolate is made. Cool, eh? The last portion of this book was written by our moms. We tried to keep their sticky fingers out of this book, but they won! Their portion is a collection of hands-on ideas that parents and educators can use to whet appetites for continued learning across the curriculum. (Can you tell that our moms told us to write that last part?) If you didn't understand, I didn't either. Really, our moms thought it would be cool to give other parents and teachers ideas as to how to make learning fun. We decided it was okay because all the ideas were covered in chocolate…of course!

What are we waiting for? Grab your apron and let's get started!

Patty

Maddy &

Sammy

Sammy's Safety Tips

1. It's important to dry your hands before touching anything electrical!

2. When cooking on top of the stove, turn the handles of the pans you are using toward the back of the stove. This will prevent someone from bumping a hot pan or spilling its contents!

3. Whenever you use a mixer or a blender, be sure to turn the appliance off and unplug it before you scrape the sides of the bowl or remove the cover.

4. Make sure you hold the plug when you pull out a cord from its outlet.

5. Be extra careful when you are working with the stove! Make sure that you turn off the burners and the oven when you're not using them.

6. Be sure to clean your mess as you go! Less clutter

in the kitchen creates a safer (and more pleasant!) place to be. Rinsing and stacking bowls, pans, and utensils in the sink as you work will make cleaning up much easier!

7. Make sure you have a few hot pads handy when you pull a treat out of the oven. Never touch the sides of a hot dish or place the dish directly on a countertop. You could easily burn yourself as well as the surface. Ouch!

8. Invite your parents to join you in the kitchen! The kitchen is a fabulous place to make memories and yummy treats.

Section 1

Cakes & CUPCAKES

Consulate

of

Cake
County

Popcorn Cake

"This is a special recipe Grandma made each year for family birthdays. It was always so fun to share our special day with her. The celebration wouldn't have been complete without this signature sweet treat! Take a minute to write a note to your grandmother or grandfather. I have a feeling that reading your note will be the highlight of their day!"

–Patty

Ingredients:

4 quarts of popped popcorn
1 pound of candy-coated chocolates
8 oz. salted peanuts
1/2 cup margarine or butter
1/2 cup oil
1 lb. marshmallows

Directions:

1. Get ready to get messy, my friend! First, you will melt the butter, oil, and marshmallows in a saucepan on low. Remove the pan from the heat once the marshmallows are completely

melted. Be sure to stir the ooey-gooey mixture often.

2. Place the popped popcorn into a bowl. Pour the hot mixture over the top. Now it's time to stir it up!

3. Add the peanuts and candy-coated chocolates soon, before the mixture begins to harden. Make sure all the ingredients are mixed thoroughly. You guessed correctly...it's Sticky Fingers Time! Pack and press your creation into a greased bundt or tube pan. Gently flip the pan onto a plate. Allow the popcorn cake to cool completely before you cut it into wedges.

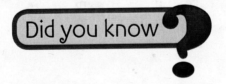

Recently, a new world record was set for creating the world's largest popcorn ball. *This gargantuan creation weighed in at a whopping 3,423 pounds!* The ball was nearly eight feet in diameter and twenty-five feet in circumference. It took several days to create the popcorn ball. Now that is a corny fact!

Myrtle Turtle Cupcakes

"You might not always agree with a sister or brother. Hey, you might even get in an argument every once in a while. That is normal. No one gets along all of the time. Even though your sister or brother may be different, you can still enjoy them for whom they are. It might even help your relationship if you work on a project (like making Myrtle Turtle Cupcakes!) or ask them for their opinion on a subject they have studied. Give em' a chance! What do you have to lose?"

–Patty

Ingredients:

1 package brownie mix, plus ingredients to prepare mix
1/3 cup chopped pecans
1 cup chocolate frosting
1/2 cup coarsely chopped pecans, toasted
18 individually wrapped caramel squares
3 tablespoons whipping cream

Directions:

1. Heat the oven to 350 degrees. Line 54 mini-muffin cups with paper liners. Read and follow directions (very carefully!) on the package of brownies. Next, stir in the chopped pecans.
2. Spoon the ooey-gooey batter into prepared muffin cups. You'll want to fill them 2/3 full.
3. Bake 18 minutes or so, cutie pie! Cool in pans on wire racks for 5 minutes. Remove cupcakes to racks; cool them completely.
4. Enjoy spreading frosting over cooled cupcakes; top each cupcake with the toasted pecans.
5. Unwrap caramels. Combine caramels and 2 tablespoons cream in small saucepan. Cook and stir over low heat until caramels are melted and mixture is smooth. Add additional 1 tablespoon cream if needed. Spoon the ooey-gooey caramel over your delicious cupcakes!

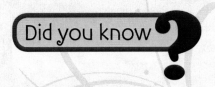

Did you know?

It would take a line of over 10 billion pecans to reach the moon. Now that's nutty!

Toppin' It Off Cupcakes

"Leaving the world a better place is everyone's responsibility! Sure, you could make these cupcakes according to the package directions. The treats would be tasty. They would also be boring. Jazzing the cakes up with peanut butter, icing, and candies makes an ordinary cupcake extraordinary! Potting a flower or planting a tree adds beauty to your surroundings. Life is fuller and more beautiful when we take an extra step toward making our world a better place."

–Patty

Ingredients:

1 package chocolate cake mix, plus ingredients to prepare mix

1 container vanilla frosting

1/2 cup creamy peanut butter

12 miniature peanut butter cup candies, wrappers removed and cut in half

Directions:

1. My friend, it's time to preheat your oven to 350 degrees. Place paper liners in 30 muffin cups.

2. Prepare, bake, and cool cupcakes following the package directions. Next, combine the vanilla frosting and peanut butter in a medium bowl. Stir all the ingredients until they are smooth.

3. I saw that! You just dipped into the creamy mixture hoping to sneak a treat! Okay, maybe it's okay to dip one time! Frost each cupcake. Decorate with peanut butter cup candy, placing the cut side down. Ooh la la!

Did you know?

The largest cake ever created weighed 128,238 pounds and 8 ounces. To frost this enormous cake, it required 16,209 pounds of icing! Whoa...that must have been one fun party! Where was my invitation?

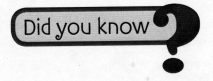

German Chocolate Pound Cake

"This popular cake is eaten all over the world but originates from the beautiful country of Germany. If you meet someone who looks different from you or speaks another language, remember that they have something special to offer. It may be a special tradition, game, or recipe from their culture. They might be willing to share a friendship with you. Everyone has something to offer. What could you share?"

—Patty

Ingredients:

1 German chocolate cake mix
1 can coconut pecan frosting
4 eggs
1/2 cup oil
1 cup water
2 tablespoons powdered sugar

Directions:

1. Okay, sweetheart, flip the dial on your oven

to 350 degrees. It's Sticky Fingers Time once again! Get your hands all messy while greasing a tube or bundt pan. Lightly dust the inside of the pan with flour. Have someone help you with this the first time. It will surely be a cinch the next time you try!

2. Dump the cake mix, frosting, oil, and water into a large bowl. Carefully crack the eggs and add them to the rest of the ingredients. Make sure that none of that nasty shell sneaks its way into the bowl, kiddo! Grab an electric mixer. Beat the ingredients on medium speed for 2 full minutes.

3. Pour the cake batter into your pan. Bake your cake for 55 to 60 minutes. Allow the cake to cool for about 10 minutes. Using hot pads, gently flip the pan over onto a plate. Once the cake is right side up, dust it with powdered sugar!

Did you know

You just used vegetable oil to make this delicious cake. This same oil can also be used as diesel fuel to run your mom's or dad's car if the vehicle is properly converted! Vegetable oil is often used to make soaps, candles, and perfumes as well. I'm not kidding—it's true!

Choc-O-Chip Bundt Cake

Ingredients:

1 box butter cake mix
3/4 cup oil
1 small box instant chocolate pudding mix
4 eggs
1/4 cup water
2 tablespoons vanilla
8 oz. sour cream
6 oz. mini morsel chocolate chips

Directions:

1. Preheat your oven to 325 degrees. Using an electric mixer, beat together the cake mix, oil, pudding mix, eggs, water, and vanilla. This should take 2 minutes or so, kiddo.
2. Next, you'll want to add the sour cream and chocolate chips. Using a spatula, gently fold in these ingredients until they are mixed through.
3. It's Sticky Fingers Time! Get your hands all messy and grease a bundt pan, my friend. Dust the greased pan with a little flour. This extra little

step will allow your cake to flip onto a plate without messing up the shape of your cake. Pour the batter into the greased pan and place the pan in the preheated oven.

4. Bake your cake for 50 to 55 minutes. Allow the cake to cool for 10 minutes. Very carefully, flip the cake onto a plate. You might ask a parent to help you with this last step. It can be a little tricky occasionally!

"Dusting the bundt pan with flour seems like a silly little step. You might wonder, *Is this really worth the extra time?* In this recipe, this little step is very important. It can make the difference of whether the cake comes out of the bundt pan cleanly or whether it gets stuck and won't come out at all! Checking over your work at school or taking the extra time to help someone out seems unnecessary sometimes. Many times, taking the extra step can make a big difference in your grades and the quality of your relationships!"

–Patty

Did you know?

Sour cream is actually cream that has soured naturally by the action of lactic-acid bacteria. Sour cream contains 18–20 percent fat. Light sour cream contains 40 percent less fat than regular sour cream because it is made from half and half.

Cocoa Cakes

Ingredients:

2 1/4 cups flour
1 tablespoon baking powder
1/2 teaspoon salt
1 2/3 cups sugar
1 cup milk
1 stick softened butter
2 tablespoons vanilla
3 egg whites, separated from yolks
1 cup crushed chocolate sandwich cookies
1 container vanilla frosting

Directions:

1. If you would like to tackle a challenge, this recipe is perfect for you, dude! Preheat your oven to 350 degrees. You know what time it is…it's Sticky Fingers Time! Grease 24 muffin pan cups.

2. Mix your flour, baking powder, and salt together in a large bowl. Stir in that sweet sugar. Add the milk, butter, and vanilla; beat with an electric mixer on a low speed for 30 seconds. Now

turn up the speed and beat it up for 2 more minutes!

3. Separating an egg yolk from the white is a bit tricky but so incredibly fun. Flip to the back of this book to find easy-to-understand instructions. Now you can add your egg whites. Beat it all up for 2 additional minutes. The crushed cookies can be dumped in now. Look at you—you are quite talented!

4. Next, spoon the batter evenly into your prepared muffin tins. Bake 20 to 25 minutes or until a toothpick inserted into the center comes out clean. Allow the cupcakes to cool in their pans on wire racks for 10 minutes. Remove the muffins then put them onto the racks to cool completely. Frost cupcakes and garnish with the crushed cookies.

"I'm impressed with how you tried something new today! Separating the eggs isn't something that most kids would attempt. Don't let challenges get in the way of trying to accomplish your dreams, kiddo. What else would you like to accomplish? Go ahead…you can do it!"

—Patty

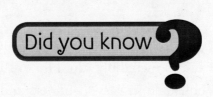

Did you know?

Salt, our oldest preservative, was extremely rare in the past. So rare, in fact, that it was often used as pay. Imagine earning a couple tablespoons of salt in exchange for cleaning your room, dusting the entire house for Mom, and helping organize the garage for Dad!

SECTION 2

Cookies
& BARS

King

OF THE

Cookie
Kingdom

Munchin' Malts

INGREDIENTS:

1 package (18 oz.) refrigerated cookie dough
1/2 cup malted milk powder
1 container chocolate frosting
1 cup chopped malted milk balls

DIRECTIONS:

1. It's time to ask a parent to help turn on the oven! Ask them (sweetly!) to preheat the oven to 350 degrees. Now the fun begins! Smear some butter on your hands and grease the cookie sheets. Remove the cookie dough from its wrapper and place it in a big mixing bowl.

2. You're learning how to measure, so the next step will be a breeze for you, whiz kid! Add 1/3 cup malted milk powder to dough in bowl. Beat with an electric mixer until the stuff is blended.

3. Dig around the kitchen until you discover a small ice cream scoop. Use this scoop to drop the dough onto the greased cookie sheets.

4. Bake 10 to 12 minutes or until cookies are

lightly browned at edges. Even though the cookies look good enough to devour, give them an extra 5 minutes to cool! Remove them from the pan and place them on wire racks to cool completely.

5. Combine the frosting and remaining 3 table-spoons malted milk powder. Top each cookie with frosting. Add a few crushed malted milk balls to the top of each cookie.

"The best part is yet to come! Take some time to chat with your parent about your day while you are munchin' on your malts."

—Sammy

Malted milkshakes were originally concocted as a health food! Malt powder was created in 1887 as an easily digested infant formula made from wheat, malted barley, and milk. Pharmacists promoted the drink as a complete meal for both infants and adults. Chocolate malt milkshakes became a wildly popular soda fountain treat during the 1920s. Malts are still quite popular today!

Nuttylicious Bars

"Consider sending a plate of treats to a neighbor. You'll find that sharing with others is quite satisfying!"

—Sammy

INGREDIENTS:

3/4 cup honey
1 cup smooth peanut butter
1 cup semi-sweet chocolate chips
10 large white marshmallows
3 cups crisp rice cereal
1 cup salted peanuts, finely chopped

DIRECTIONS:

1. It's Sticky Fingers Time! Go ahead and grease a 9 x 12 pan, superstar! Combine the honey and peanut butter in a saucepan. Flip the dial to low, stirring the honey and peanut butter

occasionally until it begins to boil. Next, you'll want to remove the saucepan to a hot pad.

2. You've finished all the tough stuff! Now add the chocolate chips and marshmallows. Stir this until it is completely melted.

3. Add the cereal and peanuts. Grease your hands slightly. Pack the peanut mixture into the pan, pressing firmly and evenly. It's a blast hanging out in the kitchen, isn't it? Chill out as your treats chill in the refrigerator. After your creation has completely cooled, you can cut them into 18 bars.

It takes twelve honeybees to produce one tablespoon of honey!

Party in a Pan!

"When something really great happens for someone else, try your best to be genuinely happy for them. Focus on their happiness rather than what hasn't happened for you. Celebrate your pal's success—that's what good friends do!"

—Sammy

INGREDIENTS:

1/4 cup chilled butter
1/2 cup smooth peanut butter
1 cup chocolate chips
8 oz. colored miniature marshmallows

DIRECTIONS:

1. It's Sticky Fingers Time! Get your hands all messy while greasing a 9 x 9 baking dish. Melt the butter and peanut butter in a saucepan over medium heat. Stir in the chocolate chips until the mixture is smooth. You can go ahead and turn the stove off. Carefully remove the saucepan from the burner. Wait about 10

minutes—the saucepan ought to be completely cool before you go to the next step.

2. Dump in the marshmallows, dude! Stir the mixture until everything is covered. Press the treats firmly in the pan with your hand. Chill out while your dessert cools down. You can cut the treats into squares. Okay, time to chow down!

DID YOU KNOW?

Originally marshmallows were made from mixing the gooey center of the marsh mallow plant (Althaea Officinalis) with sugar and honey. In the early twentieth century, the French version of the marshmallow was popularized in America. At that time, the plant portion of this sweet treat was replaced with gelatin.

P-Nut Cookies

INGREDIENTS:

1 chocolate cake mix (devil's food is super yummy!)

¾ cup crunchy peanut butter

2 eggs

2 tablespoons milk

1 cup candy-coated peanut butter pieces

DIRECTIONS:

1. Preheat the oven to 350 degrees. It's Sticky Fingers Time! Go ahead and grease two baking sheets. Lovin' getting those fingers messy? I thought so!

2. Combine the cake mix, peanut butter, eggs, and milk in a big mixing bowl. Beat the mixture on low speed with an electric mixer until all the ingredients are completely blended. It's time to stir in the peanut butter pieces!

3. Drop the cookie dough by rounded tablespoonfuls onto your baking sheets. Our treat is getting better by the minute! Bake 7 to 9 minutes or until the cookies are lightly browned. Don't

burn your tongue by eating them right away. Be sure to let the cookies cool at least 5 minutes on the baking sheets. Remove each cookie to a cooling rack until you are ready for a snack. I can tell the cookies won't be resting long, will they?

"Maybe it's time to let your parent rest for a bit. Consider helping around the house today. A simple question such as 'Is there anything I could do to make your day easier?' will please your parents and give them one more reason to appreciate you."

—Sammy

Peanuts are often used in the manufacture of dynamite. Explosive, dude!

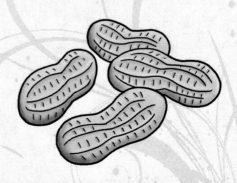

"Never-too-late for choc-o-late" Bars

"Resist the temptation to open the oven door while your candy bars are baking. Opening the door allows cold air to seep into the oven, changing the temperature inside. That temperature affects how your candy bars will taste and how long they will have to bake. Flipping on the oven light is a great way to watch your treats bake. Patience is a beautiful quality, my friend!"

—Sammy

INGREDIENTS:

1 cup brown sugar
1/2 cup sugar
3/4 cup crunchy peanut butter
1 stick softened butter
2 eggs
1 teaspoon vanilla
1/4 cup milk
1 3/4 cups flour
1 teaspoon baking powder
1 package candy-coated peanut butter pieces

1/3 cup chopped peanuts

1 container chocolate frosting

DIRECTIONS:

1. Be sure to preheat your oven to 325 degrees. It's Sticky Fingers Time! Smear some butter on a 13 x 9 inch baking pan.
2. Beat the sugars, peanut butter, and butter in large bowl with an electric mixer on medium speed until the mixture is creamy. Add eggs and vanilla; beat until fluffy. Ooh la la! Gradually beat in milk. Carefully add both the flour and baking powder, beating until it is well blended. Stir in 1 cup of the peanut butter candies and nuts.
3. Spread into your prepared pan. Bake 40 minutes or so. Let the dessert cool completely. Next, spread frosting over the top! Sprinkle the entire dessert with remaining candies. Carefully use a knife to cut your dessert into bars.

DID YOU KNOW?

Butter was discovered by Arabs on their travels. Flasks of milk got shaken up by the motion of their camels. This shaking made a glob of fat rise to the top. This was the start of the "spreadable gold" that most of us enjoy!

Oat Chocochippers

(Oats...Does that mean it's good for me?)

INGREDIENTS:

1 package yellow cake mix
1 teaspoon baking powder
3/4 cup vegetable oil
2 eggs
2 teaspoons vanilla
1 cup uncooked old-fashioned oats
1 1/2 cups mini chocolate chips

DIRECTIONS:

1. It's time to ask someone to help turn on the oven to 350 degrees. It's Sticky Fingers Time! Lightly grease two cookie sheets.

2. The next step is really important! Stir together the cake mix and baking powder in a large bowl. Make sure it is mixed through completely. If you find a clump of baking powder in your cookies, you will know it! Nasty, that is for certain! Add the oil, eggs, and vanilla. Take

a minute to stir all the ingredients together. Dump the oats and chocolate chips into the bowl and mix it all up!

3. Drop the dough by heaping tablespoons onto the cookie sheets. Leave about 2 inches between each cookie. Place the cookies into the oven and bake them for 10 to 12 minutes. Allow your Chocochippers to cool on the cookie sheets for 5 to 10 minutes. Remove the cookies to a wire rack to cool completely.

"If your parents helped out with the masterpiece you just made, ask them to tell you a humorous story from their childhood. You might want to share a funny story as well! Giggle together—it's just as healthy as the oats are for your body!"

—Sammy

DID YOU KNOW?

Oatmeal Month is celebrated each January, the month in which we buy more oatmeal than any other month of the year. In recent years, we have stocked our pantries with over 35 million pounds of oats. That is enough oats to fill 346 million bowls of oatmeal! Just hearing that fact makes me feel full!

Colossal Cake Cookies

"This recipe brings back fabulous memories! My friends would come over, and we would make these cookies together. It's been a while since I've contacted these friends…maybe I'll pick up the phone and call them sometime soon. Keeping up with old friends is a gift you continue to give and receive. Go ahead—pick up your phone and dial!"

—Sammy

INGREDIENTS:

1 package chocolate cake mix
1/3 cup water
1/4 cup butter, softened
1 egg
1 1/2 cups white chocolate chips
1/2 cup chopped walnuts

DIRECTIONS:

1. Preheat your oven to 350 degrees, sweetheart!

It's Sticky Fingers Time, so grease two cookie sheets. Combine cake mix, water, butter, and egg in large bowl. Beat with electric mixer on medium speed until all the ingredients are well mixed. Go ahead and stir in the chips and nuts. It's so easy, isn't it?

2. Using an ice cream scoop, drop the large heaps of dough 5 inches apart onto prepared cookie sheets.

3. Bake 15 to 17 minutes or until the cookies are set. Let cookies stand on cookie sheets for 5 minutes. Because these cookies are so big, be super careful when you remove them to wire racks to cool.

DID YOU KNOW?

More than 87,000,000,000 eggs are produced in the U.S. each year. Check out all those zeros...whoa!

SECTION 3

Frozen
TREATS

Guru
OF
Glacial
Goodies

Chocoalamondo Shake

"It's easy to double this recipe and share the Chocoalamondo shakes with your buddies. Now that is one sure way to make friends and influence people!"

~Maddy

INGREDIENTS:

1 cup milk
7 scoops vanilla ice cream
1/4 cup chocolate syrup
1/4 cup almond butter

DIRECTIONS:

Using the highest setting on your blender, mix all the ingredients for 1 minute. Depending on how you like to enjoy your shakes, add additional milk (to make it thinner) or ice cream (to make it thicker). It's as easy as it can be!

DID YOU KNOW?

Almonds are actually "stones," not nuts. These stones are the ones found in the middle of the fruit, like peach stones, and not the ones you pick up from the ground. Cool, huh?

Nanachocolicious Pops

"Can you say the name of this recipe three times really fast? I won't tell you how delicious these pops are. I won't mention how nutritious they are either. Go ahead and find out for yourself!"

~Maddy

INGREDIENTS:

5 small ripe bananas
4 cartons banana yogurt (8 oz. each)
1/2 teaspoon nutmeg
1/2 teaspoon cinnamon
1 cup mini chocolate chips

DIRECTIONS:

1. Carefully slice the banana, placing it in a blender with the yogurt, nutmeg, and cinnamon. Blend

until smooth. Transfer your creation to a small bowl. Stir in the chocolate chips.

2. Spoon banana mixture into plastic popsicle molds. Carefully place tops on each of the molds. Set the molds in the provided stand. Don't worry if you don't have the molds; you can use ice cube trays and popsicle sticks. Set on a level surface in the freezer. Freeze at least 3 hours until firm.

3. When you are ready for a treat, briefly run warm water over the molds until each pop loosens.

"Enjoy your creation! Be sure to thank your parent for helping you as you made this yummy treat. Being extra sweet may persuade your parent to help with cleanup as well. Having and using manners has its privileges."

~Maddy

DID YOU KNOW

If you peel a banana from the bottom, you won't have to pick the little "stringy things" off it. That's how primates eat their bananas. They don't monkey around!

Hands Off My Malt!

"This malt is simple to prepare yet so delicious! Sometimes 'simple' is best. Be kind. Be honest. Be respectful. Be yourself. Others will respect you for acting this way and being this type of person. It's really rather simple, isn't it?"

~Maddy

INGREDIENTS:

1 cup milk

7 scoops of ice cream (chocolate, vanilla, and cookie dough are super good choices!)

5 tablespoons instant malted milk powder (or 15 malted milk balls)

DIRECTIONS:

Digging out the blender from the cupboard

is the toughest part of making this recipe! Just blend all the ingredients for 1 minute. Depending on how you like to enjoy your shakes, add additional milk (to make it thinner) or ice cream (to make it thicker). It's amazing how good three ingredients can be!

To this day, the history of ice cream remains a mystery. However, many say this treat is credited to Emperor Nero of Rome. It was a mixture of snow, nectar, fruit pulp, and honey. Others proclaim that Marco Polo, a thirteenth century adventurer, brought ice cream to Europe from the Far East. Regardless of where it came from, today's average American consumes over 24 quarts of ice cream each year. Impress your friends with those facts!

Wafflelicious Ice Cream Towers

"Burning chocolate is easy to do! The manufacturer of the hot fudge topping knows how to best prepare their product. The chocolate tastes much better if you pay attention to their simple suggestions. Similarly, your parents have certain household rules and expectations. They love you dearly and want the very best for you. Paying attention to and following their guidelines will help you to become a fantastic adult."

~Maddy

INGREDIENTS:

4 frozen waffles
1/4 cup hot fudge
4 large scoops of your favorite ice cream
aerosol whipped cream
colored sprinkles

Directions:

1. Okay, let's get started! Heat the waffles in your toaster until they are golden brown.
2. Next, you'll want to heat the fudge topping in your handy dandy microwave. You'll want to read the directions on the back of the jar. Remember—chocolate can burn easily, so don't overheat our liquid gold, dude!
3. Place one waffle on each of four plates. Scoop your ice cream, placing a scoop on each waffle. Drizzle the hot fudge topping over the top. Have some fun decorating each tower with whipped cream and sprinkles.

DID YOU KNOW

Believe it or not, March 25 is International Waffle Day! Yes, you heard it right. The U.S. also has a holiday dedicated to this tasty treat on August 24. Wacky, eh?

Homemade Ice Cream Sandwiches

INGREDIENTS:

20 store-bought chocolate chip cookies
1 bag mini chocolate chips
10 scoops ice cream (chocolate or vanilla)

DIRECTIONS:

1. You will *love* this easy recipe! Sandwich a scoop of ice cream between two cookies. Roll the sides in the chocolate mini baking bits.
2. Individually wrap your creations in plastic wrap and store them in the freezer.

"Be sure to clean up the mess in the kitchen after you are finished. Your parents will be proud as

they see you being independent and acting respon-
sible. I must say, pretty impressive!"

~Maddy

DID YOU KNOW

The average single scoop of ice cream takes nearly
fifty licks to finish. You might just have to try this
little experiment at home!

NanaSplit Shake

"After you have mastered this recipe and can successfully work the blender, you might want to teach a little brother or sister how to make the NanaSplit Shake. Believe it or not, your younger siblings look up to you. They would *love* to learn how to do the things you are able to do!"

~Maddy

INGREDIENTS:

1 cup milk
7 scoops vanilla ice cream
6 fresh strawberries
1 large banana
1/4 cup chocolate syrup

DIRECTIONS:

This one is a snap! Ask a parent to help you find the blender. Allow them to show you how to use it. Blend all the ingredients for 1 minute. Depending on how you like to enjoy your shakes, add additional milk (to make it thinner) or ice cream (to make it thicker). It's as easy as it can be! Slurp it through a straw and enjoy your creation! Excellent work, chef!

DID YOU KNOW

The largest strawberry ever grown weighed half a pound. That is one huge berry, kiddo!

Chocolate-covered Strawberry Shake-up

"All these ingredients are quite different, but when mixed together, they blend to make one flavorful and fantastic treat. When choosing your friends, be sure to include all different types of people. Some may like music, others play sports, yet others may like to draw. You'll find that time spent with various types of people allows for more interesting friendships. Try it out!"

~Maddy

INGREDIENTS:

1 1/2 cups milk
2 cups whipped cream
7 large scoops of strawberry ice cream
10 large strawberries
1/2 cup chocolate syrup

Directions:

Blend these ingredients for 1 to 2 minutes. Depending on how you like to enjoy your shakes, add additional milk (to make it thinner) or ice cream (to make it thicker). It's as easy as it can be! Pour your Shake-up into a tall glass. Simply delicious!

DID YOU KNOW?

Strawberries are the only fruit with seeds on the outside. Believe it or not, the average berry has two hundred seeds!

Section 4

Specialty
DESSERTS

Duchess

of

Desirable
Desserts

Chocolate Soup

"You won't need much help today, my little chef! Measuring is the biggest challenge this time. For you, it's probably no challenge at all, Einstein!"

–Patty

Ingredients:

1/4 cup unsweetened cocoa powder
2 tablespoons cornstarch
1 1/2 cups whole milk
1/3 cup sugar
2 teaspoons vanilla
1/8 teaspoon cinnamon

Directions:

1. Combine cocoa and cornstarch in a medium-sized microwave-safe bowl, kiddo.
2. Carefully add the milk, stirring it with a wire whisk until it is blended.
3. Microwave for 2 minutes. Stir it up, my friend! Microwave for 4 minutes, stirring every 1½ minutes or so.
4. We're almost finished! Go ahead and stir in

the sugar, vanilla, and cinnamon. Let the soup stand at least 5 minutes before serving. You can slurp this pudding through a straw, use a spoon, or if your parents are on board, eat it with no utensils at all!

"Your parent may have had a long, stressful day at work. Believe it or not, sometimes adults want to act like kids. Your parent may want to join you as you slurp your chocolate soup through a straw. What a blast that could be!"

–Patty

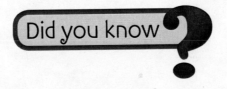

It takes about 10 pounds of milk to make one pound of cheese. The average cow produces 2,000 pounds of milk in a month, or 210 pounds of cheese. By the way, that same cow can produce about 46,000 glasses of milk in a year!

Red Carpet Truffles

"Truffles are often served in fancy restaurants and are prized for the way they are displayed. We spend a lot of time picking out our clothes, trying to look our best each morning. Have you taken the time to develop a beautiful person on your 'inside'? Are you loyal, trustworthy, kind, and generous to others? Just like truffles, it's what's on the inside that matters most!"

–Patty

Ingredients:

1 (18 oz.) package of chocolate sandwich cookies

1 (8 oz.) package cream cheese, softened

1 1/2 cups semi-sweet chocolate chips

1/2 cup peanut butter, mint, or cherry-flavored chocolate chips

3 tablespoons shortening

Directions:

1. You will surely make a statement on the runway with these beautiful truffles! Ask a parent to crush the sandwich cookies in a food processor. You can dump the cookie crumbs into a large mixing bowl. Add the softened cream cheese to the same bowl. Use an electric mixer on medium speed to combine the ingredients. Your mixture will be super stiff once it is thoroughly mixed.

2. Pull out a large cookie sheet and cut a piece of wax paper to fit its length. Use a mini scoop to make uniform balls. Roll the balls of dough in your hands to make them smooth. Place all of the truffles on the lined cookie sheet. Find a level spot in your freezer for the truffles. After you've given the balls a chance to harden (about 45 minutes in the freezer), take them out and set them on your countertop.

3. Pour the semi-sweet chocolate chips and 2 tablespoons of shortening into a tall glass measuring cup. Place them in the microwave for 1 minute. Stir it up, cutie! If the mixture is still lumpy, return the chocolate to the microwave for another 30 seconds. Stir the chocolate until it is completely smooth. Dunk the truffles into the chocolate, allowing them to be completely

drenched. Place a fork under the truffle and gently remove it from the chocolate and place it back on the wax paper. Repeat these steps until all the truffles are covered in chocolate.

4. Combine the flavored chips and shortening in small re-sealable plastic food storage bag. Seal the bag. Microwave on high for 30 seconds. Squish the bag lightly. If you need to, microwave for an additional 15 seconds until chips and shortening are completely melted and smooth. Knead bag after each 15 second interval. Cut off a tiny corner of the bag. Drizzle this melted, flavored chocolate over the chocolate-covered truffles using a criss-cross pattern. Fancy, huh? Place the completed truffles into a covered container. Make sure the truffles don't touch one another! When you are ready to serve your Red Carpet Truffles, place them neatly on a raised cake plate, giving them stardom status!

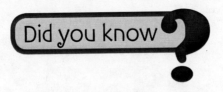

Did you know?

A chocolate bar contains more calcium, protein, and B2 vitamin than a banana or an orange!

Hazelnut S'mores

"Could this new type of S'more be as good as the original? Find out for yourself! Be willing to try new things! Many of these recipes could be altered by your creativity. Professional chefs try out new recipes all the time. They often change the ingredients to make the classic recipe more unique. Branch out—I bet you will love the results!"

—Patty

Ingredients:

16 graham crackers
1 jar chocolate hazelnut spread
8 large white marshmallows

Directions:

1. Welcome back, kiddo! It's time to get started. First, use a knife to spread all sixteen graham crackers with some chocolate hazelnut spread. Next, place two of the crackers on a plate. Place the marshmallows on top.

2. Microwave on high for 15 seconds. Carefully remove the plate from the microwave.

3. Finally, place the other two crackers on top of each marshmallow. Push down slightly until the marshmallows spread easily. Repeat this process until all the ingredients are finished. This makes a fantastic after-school snack!

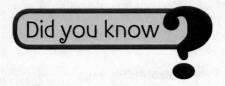

Did you know?

Have you ever wondered why the famous campfire treat was named S'more? Many people believe the name was given because once they finished gobbling the treat, most people asked for "some more please!" Hmm...now that makes sense!

More S'mores Please!

Ingredients:

1 package (18 oz.) refrigerated chocolate chip cookie dough
1/3 cup graham cracker crumbs
3 cups mini marshmallows
1 1/2 cups milk chocolate chips
4 tablespoons shortening

Directions:

1. Flip the dial on the oven to 350 degrees. Dig inside your cabinets to find a 13 x 9 inch baking dish. It's Sticky Fingers Time! Go ahead and grease the pan, kiddo.

2. Next, remove the cookie dough from its wrapper. I know what you are thinking: *That cookie dough sure looks delicious!* Resist the temptation to nibble, as the dough contains raw eggs. You could easily get one big belly ache! Press the dough into your prepared pan. Sprinkle the graham cracker crumbs over the dough.

3. Bake 10 to 12 minutes. The marshmallows come next. Go ahead and sprinkle them on top. Place your dish back in the oven and bake for 2 to 3 minutes more. Allow your treat to cool completely on a wire rack.

4. Okay, the next step is really cool. Have some fun with this! You may even teach your mom and dad this trick! Combine chocolate chips and shortening in small re-sealable plastic food storage bag. Seal the bag. Microwave on high for 1 minute. Squish the bag lightly. If you need to, microwave for an additional 30 seconds until chips and shortening are completely melted and smooth. Knead bag after each 30 second interval. Cut off a small corner of the bag. Drizzle chocolate over bars.

5. Refrigerate 5 to 10 minutes or until chocolate is set.

"Make a memory, man! More than likely, a parent helped make these ooey-gooey S'mores. I have a feeling both of you are covered in chocolate and you had a great time together. Ask someone to take a picture of the two of you. Pictures are a great way to recreate good feelings and remember special times. So, snap away!"

–**Patty**

Did you know?

The graham cracker was originally developed as a health food that was good for digestion. This treat was named after Sylvester Graham, a preacher and nutrition expert in early nineteenth century.

Won't Budge For Fudge!

"Sharing experiences with a friend makes every experience better! Call a buddy of yours and make plans to bake together next time. You might even have your friend bring half the ingredients and send them home with a plate full of treats. Good times!"

–Patty

Ingredients:

1 1/2 cups sugar
1 cup marshmallow crème
1/2 cup evaporated milk
1/3 cup creamy peanut butter
1/2 teaspoon salt
1 (6 oz.) package of semi-sweet chocolate chips
1 teaspoon vanilla

Directions:

1. It's Sticky Fingers Time! Grease an 8 inch square

pan. It's time to combine the sugar, marshmallow crème, milk, peanut butter, and salt in large saucepan. My little chef, it's important to stir this mixture constantly over low heat until it is blended and the mixture comes to a boil.

2. Let it boil for 5 minutes, stirring it the entire time. When your 5 minutes are up, remove your pan from the heat. Add the chocolate chips, and stir until it is blended. Stir in the vanilla next.

3. You are almost finished! Pour your creation into that greasy 8 inch pan, letting it cool. Cut the fudge in small squares. Okay, maybe a little bigger! If you don't happen to eat all of the fudge, go ahead and store the remaining treats in a covered container.

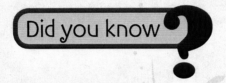

The entire vanilla cultivation process, from planting to market, usually takes from five to six years!

Peanut Butter Whirlwind Fudge

"Fudge is fabulous—super rich and sweet. A tiny one-inch square is a perfect treat that satisfies a sweet tooth. Remember...more isn't always better. You might have a friend that lives in a bigger house and owns every toy sold on the market. Having a bunch of 'stuff' doesn't necessarily make someone happier or more satisfied. Enjoy what you have been blessed with, kiddo!"

–Patty

Ingredients:

1 1/2 cups sugar
2/3 cup (5 oz. can) evaporated milk
2 tablespoons butter
1 1/2 cups miniature marshmallows
1 cup peanut butter chips
1 cup milk chocolate chips
1 teaspoon vanilla

Directions:

1. Okay, kiddo! I'm glad you're joining me in the

kitchen once again. Find some aluminum foil and line an 8 x 8 inch baking pan with it. It's Sticky Fingers Time! Take a minute to butter the foil. Set this prepared pan aside, my friend.

2. Combine the sugar, evaporated milk, and butter in a saucepan. Heat over medium heat, stirring constantly, until it reaches a full rolling boil. Keep stirring, cutie! This mixture could burn really easily. Allow the mixture to boil for 5 minutes. You did it! Remove your pan from the heat. Now it is time to stir in your marshmallows, chips, and vanilla. Continue stirring until all the marshmallows are completely melted. Pour the fudge into the pan you prepared earlier.

3. Place the pan into the refrigerator for at least 2 hours.

4. Cut your fudge into small squares. You'll want to store your treats in a tightly covered container in the refrigerator.

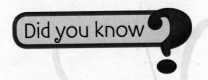

Did you know?

Evaporated milk is fresh homogenized milk with 60 percent of its water removed by evaporation. It contains 7.9 percent milk fat. It takes about 2.1 pounds of whole milk to make 1 pound of evaporated milk.

Luscious...Layer Upon Layer!

"My friend Marie recently shared this recipe. She is like a grandma to me. She is such a treasure! You don't have to be related to someone in order to love them like family. Take time to develop relationships with elderly individuals. You never know—they may become like family to you!"

–Patty

Ingredients:

Crust:
- 1 1/4 cups flour
- 1 stick butter (room temperature)
- 1/2 cup chopped pecans

Layers:
- 1 (8 oz.) package cream cheese, softened
- 1 cup powdered sugar
- 1 large container whipped topping
- 2 small packages instant milk chocolate pudding
- 3 cups milk

Directions:

Okay, partner! Mix all the ingredients for the crust. Press this mixture into a greased 9 x 13 pan.

Next you'll want to preheat your oven to 350 degrees. Bake the crust for 20 minutes. Don't over-bake this, my friend! Allow the crust to cool completely.

Mix the cream cheese, sugar, and half of the whipped topping together. Spread this creamed mixture on the crust. Using an electric mixer on medium speed, mix the pudding and milk together until the mixture is firmly set (about 2 minutes). Spread the pudding on top of the cream cheese mixture. You are almost finished, pal! Top the entire dessert with the remainder of the whipped topping. Ooh la la!

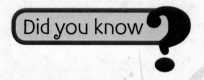

Did you know?

White chocolate is derived from the cocoa plant because it has cocoa butter in it. Yet white chocolate isn't actually considered chocolate. According to the FDA, chocolate must contain chocolate solids from the cocoa plant. These solids impart rich and intense chocolate flavor and color found in both milk and dark chocolate. False advertising, dude!

Dog-Gone-It...
These are good!

Bones for Man's Best Friend

"Your dog will love you forever once you serve these treats! So go ahead, 'Dog-gone-it,' and make your best friend happy today! Dog treats make excellent gifts for friends who love their furry friends. When your dog's birthday rolls around, making treats for the other dogs in the neighborhood would be a fun way to celebrate!"

–Patty

Ingredients:

4 cups flour
1/2 cup nonfat dry milk
1/4 cup crunchy peanut butter
1/3 cup carob chips (not chocolate chips!)
1/3 cup peanut butter chips (containing no cocoa!)
1/2 teaspoon baking powder
1/2 teaspoon salt

1/3 cup low-sodium beef or chicken bouillon powder
2 large eggs
1 cup warm water

Directions:

1. Preheat your oven to 350 degrees, sweetheart!
2. Mix all the dry ingredients (flour, dry milk, carob chips, baking powder, salt, and bouillon powder) in a large bowl. Slowly add the peanut butter, warm water, and eggs. Mix all the ingredients. The dough should be stiff like pizza dough. If it is too gloppy, add more flour!
3. Use your hands to knead the dough until it is smooth. Next, you'll want to form the dough into one gargantuan ball!
4. Place the ball on a floured surface, kiddo. Roll that dough out to 1/3 inch thick. Use a dog bone-shaped cookie cutter to cut through the dough.
5. Place the bones onto a greased cookie sheet and bake these treats for 16 to 18 minutes (or until golden brown). Remove the cookie sheets from the oven. Using a spatula, flip the bones over. Return the treats to the oven for 5 additional minutes.
6. Once all the cookies have been baked, turn off the oven. Leave the treats in the cooling oven for several hours.

You're probably wondering, *Why did we keep the bones in the oven?* This last step allows the bones to become crispy and crunchy. Your best friend will thank you for all your hard work!

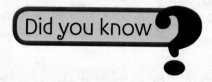

Did you know?

Each time you make one of the recipes within *Covered in Chocolate*, your canine friend probably looks at you with big puppy dog eyes. He or she is hoping to score a serving of your newest creation. It's important to know that chocolate is very bad for dogs. Chocolate contains dangerous ingredients for canines. The cocoa bean has allergy–producing anti-bodies and a caffeine stimulant called Theobromine. This stimulant can be fatal to some dogs.

Carob tastes much like chocolate but contains none of these dangerous ingredients. Carob comes from the fruit of an evergreen tree native to the Mediterranean region. The tree's large, long, bean-like pods are picked, dried, then ground into a fine powder that looks and tastes very similar to cocoa. The best part—you don't have to worry about it making your canine friend "sick as a dog!"

SECTION 5

Bonbons &
CANDY
CLUSTERS

THE

Bonbon Baron

"Nutty" about Chocolate!

"There are many people who work hard every day so that your life is made better and easier. It's important to be thoughtful to others so they feel appreciated. You might want to box up a few clusters for the individual who delivers your mail or trims your hair!"

—Sammy

INGREDIENTS:

1 1/2 cups peanut butter
1 1/2 cups milk chocolate chips
2 tablespoons shortening
4 cups peanuts

DIRECTIONS:

1. You are gonna love this one! Place chips, peanut butter, and shortening in a microwave-safe bowl. Microwave on high for 1 minute. If you need to, microwave on high an additional 15

seconds, stirring each time after heating. Chips should melt and mixture should be smooth after stirring. Go ahead and stir in the peanuts, kiddo!

2. Spoon heaping teaspoons of peanut mixture into 1 inch paper candy cups or paper-lined muffin cups. Try not to lick your fingers! I saw that!

3. Stick these treats in the refrigerator for 1 hour or until firm. Okay, now it's a great time to eat your creation. Now that you are finished, it's time to get out of the kitchen! Go read a book or head outdoors to play! If you have leftovers, be sure to store them, covered tightly, in the refrigerator.

DID YOU KNOW?

More than half the peanuts grown every year are made into peanut butter. Guess who eats most of that peanut butter? Adults!

An Edible Turtle?

INGREDIENTS:

50 individually wrapped caramel squares
3 tablespoons milk
2 cups chopped pecans
2 cups semi-sweet chocolate chips

DIRECTIONS:

1. This recipe is one of my favorites! Turtles just may be your favorite food once you've made them. First, you'll want to unwrap the caramels and put them into a saucepan. Next, you will add the milk. Heat the caramels on low. Be sure to stir the mixture often until it is completely melted.

2. Now it is time to spread waxed paper over your entire cookie sheet. Your turtles will want to stick, so be sure to grease the paper well. Mix the pecans into the melted caramel sauce. Stir it up, friend! Keep the sauce on very low heat. Drop by tablespoons onto the waxed paper. Place the caramels in the refrigerator for 2 hours.

3. You're almost finished, kiddo! Dump the chocolate chips into a microwave-safe bowl. Using the defrost option on your microwave, melt your

chips for about 1 minute or so. Stir the chips until they are melted and smooth. If the chips aren't smooth after you have stirred, place them back into the microwave, repeating the same steps. Drop one clump of caramel mixture at a time into the chocolate. Slide a spatula under the candy and lift up to let the excess chocolate drip back into the bowl. Repeat with the remaining pieces. Once your caramels have been dipped, place each one back onto the waxed paper. Chill out as your edible turtles cool!

"Chilling out isn't necessarily 'wasting time.' After working hard, it's important to take time to relax. So go ahead, daydream!"

—Sammy

DID YOU KNOW

Caramel is made by boiling sugar slowly to approximately 340 degrees Fahrenheit. As the sugar liquefies and draws near this temperature, the sugar breaks down into composites with the characteristic caramel color and flavor. Whoa! Cool, man!

Peanut Candy

"Have you ever gone outside on a rainy day, splashing in water puddles or making mud pies? It's a great time! Next time the rain begins to pour, ask your parent to join you for some fun. Your parent might be looking for a change from their normal routine. Life is a series of memories. Make a memory today while making this fun snack...dive in and have a blast!"

—Sammy

INGREDIENTS:

2/3 cup smooth peanut butter
3/4 cup granola cereal
1/3 cup skim milk powder
1 tablespoon brown sugar
1/2 cup mini chocolate chips
1/2 cup graham cracker crumbs

DIRECTIONS:

1. It's time to roll up your sleeves, as we're going to get messy! First, place the peanut butter into

a medium-sized bowl. Go ahead and add the cereal, milk powder, and brown sugar.

2. Add the chocolate chips. Mix well. Shape the dough into 1 inch balls.
3. Place the graham cracker crumbs into a small bowl. Roll the balls in the coating. Let your candy cool then place it into a covered container. Take it easy while your candy chills in the refrigerator.

DID YOU KNOW?

Chocolate has been applauded for its value as an energy source. Think of it this way: a single chocolate chip provides sufficient food energy for an adult to walk 150 feet. Hence, it would take about thirty-five chips to walk a mile, or 875,000 to take a hike around the world. Let's see…that might be a trek worth taking if I get to eat that much chocolate!

Kaboodle Moodles

INGREDIENTS:

1/2 cup butter (real butter is best!)
2 cups sugar
1/2 cup milk
7 tablespoons cocoa powder
3 cups quick-cooking rolled oats (not instant)
1/2 cup medium coconut
1/2 cup chopped walnuts
just a pinch of salt
2 teaspoons vanilla

DIRECTIONS:

1. Are you ready for another adventure in the kitchen? Go ahead and place the butter, sugar, and milk into a saucepan. If you don't feel comfortable with using the stove yet, be sure to ask a parent to help you. At medium heat you should stir often, until the mixture comes to a boil. Remove the saucepan to a hot pad.

2. Add the remaining six ingredients. Stir it up

well, my friend! Drop by rounded tablespoon-fuls onto waxed paper. Allow them to cool completely. Store covered in a container with waxed paper between the layers.

"As you polish off another treat, take a minute to think how smart you have become! So many people are quite proud of you!"

—Sammy

DID YOU KNOW

Falling coconuts kill 150 people each year. That is ten times the number of people killed by sharks. Now that is one dangerous fruit! Or is it a nut? Maybe it's a seed. Take a minute to research—you'll be surprised!

Joys

"This recipe was borrowed from my friend, Courtney. My life is sweeter now that she is my friend. I think I'll call her and tell her that today. It's one thing to *think* about saying a thoughtful word to someone, but *actually* saying it is much more important. Now is the best time to tell someone you care for them!"

— Sammy

INGREDIENTS:

1 bag coconut (14 oz.)
1 cup light corn syrup
Chocolate Coating:
4 cups chocolate chips (24 oz.)
3 tablespoons shortening

DIRECTIONS:

1. Okay, this recipe is amazing! My mouth is watering just thinking about these sweet treats! First, mix the coconut and syrup well and form into balls using a small scoop. Be sure to wet your hands with water and roll balls smooth. You'll

find that without wet hands, the coconut mixture will stick to your skin, making this task a little tricky. Trust me! Place the balls into the freezer until they harden.

2. Melt chocolate chips and shortening in your microwave, stirring the chocolate until it is smooth.

3. When your coconut balls are firm, dip the balls into the chocolate coating mixture. Licking your fingers will be a strong temptation! You may want to add an almond on top of the candy before or after coating with the chocolate, depending on whether you like nuts or not.

4. Return the goodies to the freezer to harden. You can store the Joys in an airtight container in the freezer, that is, if you don't eat them all at once!

Which is oldest?

A. Margarine
B. Butter
C. Shortening

Shortening was developed in 1905.
Margarine has only been around a little longer, since around 1870.
Butter is the oldest, as it was invented before 1800!

How is
CHOCOLATE
made, anyway?

Let's take a peek inside a
chocolate factory.

Okay, so we've given you some crazy fun facts about the ingredients within our recipes. I've got another fact that will surely surprise you. Here goes, kiddos! Chocolate actually comes from trees! Believe it or not, it's true. Honestly, there is a tree that is named a cacao tree. These trees are only found within twenty degrees of the Equator. People reach really high to pick the pods off the cacao tree. Next, they scoop out the beans that are inside the pods. These beans hold the main ingredient of chocolate.

The next step is to clean and dry the beans. The cocoa beans are stuffed into sacks and sent to the various chocolate factories. At the factory, the beans are cooked. The cooled beans are shipped to a mill. Here they are ground into a liquid. This liquid may look like chocolate, but it tastes nothing like chocolate! Trust us on this!

The chocolatier then adds sugar, milk, and cocoa butter to make the chocolate taste extra good! They sure know how to do it, because we've never tasted anything nearly as good! The liquid chocolate is then poured into molds. Over a period of time, the chocolate hardens. It becomes the same shape as the mold! You can mold the chocolate into most any shape! Cool, eh?

Large companies use massive machines to put wrappers on the chocolate. Boutique confectionaries have their own employees place the chocolate directly into the boxes. The boxes are beautifully wrapped and sent to stores around the world! Our part in the process comes next—we beg and plead for a parent to purchase the sweet treats!

APPETITE
for Learning

Mixing our love for chocolate
with the goal of learning!

1. You have just been hired as a consultant for Lindt, a prestigious Swiss chocolate company. Your assignment is to create a new chocolate bar. Be sure to address the following questions: What is the name of the candy bar? What will it taste like? What will the new bar look like? How will the packaging look? How will you decide to market this new treat? Good luck!

2. Did you know that cacao pods are grown in regions twenty degrees from the Equator? Grab a map and take a few minutes to find the countries within this area. Take this opportunity to study the land features and cultures of these regions!

3. Create a web to represent the rainforest ecosystem. Once the web is created, take away various pieces of the ecosystem to demonstrate the interconnectedness of the system.

4. Did you know that the dried cocoa bean became a form of currency? At one time several important Central American civilizations began to develop a financial system in which the cocoa bean was used as the basis for accounting. The standard measure of the Mayan culture was the "carga." This was equivalent to the load of beans one man could carry on his

back (approximately 8,000 beans). Learn more about this unique financial system.

5. Read about the process of making chocolate. Create a diagram showing the process of converting cacao to the various edible forms of chocolate. Transfer your information to a poster board for display.

6. Enjoy reading *Cam Jansen and the Chocolate Fudge Mystery* by David A. Adler. Consider rewriting the last chapter. Perhaps another twist? Perhaps a different ending?

7. Make two lists:

   • Create a list of words (pertaining to chocolate of course!) that you'd like to learn to spell.

   • Create a list of vocabulary terms that you'd like to learn. For example: roasting, milling, alkalization, molding, etc.

8. Look for Janet S. Redhead's book, *The Big Block of Chocolate*. Rewrite this story using different characters (a horse, an elephant, or perhaps a cat).

9. Chocolate sure is tasty—we all know that! A growing number of physicians are recognizing the healthy components of this delicious treat. Do some research. Are there any health benefits

from consuming chocolate? I'll cross my fingers and hope that chocolate will be one of the main food groups someday!

10. Head to your local library and find the book *Chocolatina* by Erik Kraft. Enjoy reading!

11. Enjoy eating your favorite chocolate candy bar. Save the wrapper to examine the ingredients. Learn more about the ingredients themselves to see whether this is a healthy treat or not.

12. Peek inside your local library to find Margret Rey's book *Curious George Goes to a Chocolate Factory.*

13. Learn the changes made to chocolate throughout the centuries with regards to consumption. Chart your research on a timeline.

14. Read *The Chocolate Train* by Joanne Kornfield.

15. Make a recipe within this cookbook. Brainstorm ways in which you might improve upon the recipe. Create your very own version of the recipe. Be sure to write down all the steps in a precise manner so that you can share your special recipe with others!

16. Read *Chocolate: Riches from the Rainforest* by Robert Burleigh.

17. Try a science experiment together!

    • Find out whether it is best to use hot or cold water when making cocoa. Should you heat the water before adding the cocoa mix, or should you heat your drink after you completed stirring the cocoa?

    • What will you need? Two mugs, your favorite cocoa mix, and two spoons.

    • What will you do? Fill one mug with hot water. Fill the second mug with cold water. Add three heaping tablespoons of cocoa mix to each mug. Stir.

    • This experiment demonstrates spaces in water molecules. If you would like to research why one method works best, you can study this chemistry concept more in depth. Go ahead—dive in!

18. Check out *Max's Chocolate Chicken* by Rosemary Wells from your local library.

19. Check out the book entitled *M&M Math* from your local library. Eat a few M&Ms along the way—the learning is so much sweeter!

20. Play Chocolate Bingo with your brother or sister. Use chocolate chips as your markers!

21. Read *Is There a Cure for Chocolate Fever?* by Robert Kimmel Smith.

22. If you could write your own book about chocolate, what might happen in the story?

23. Read *The Chocolate Cow* by Lilian Obligado.

24. Watch the video and read the book *Charlie and the Chocolate Factory* with a parent. Compare and contrast the two, making a list of similarities and differences.

25. Learn how a pharmacist in the 1860s revolutionized the chocolate industry. Which pharmacist should you study? None other than Henri Nestle!

26. Take a look at the book entitled *The Chocolate Touch* by Patrick Skene Catling.

27. Learn about the metric system. How does it compare to the measurement system that we commonly use in America?

28. Research when, where, why, and by whom chocolate was first introduced, received, planted, harvested, used, and changed.

29. Enjoy reading *A Chocolate Moose for Dinner* by Fred Gwynne.

30. Write a poem! Use chocolate as your inspiration!

31. Study the Swiss chocolate pioneers! Here are a few names you'll want to include in your study:

- Francois-Louis Cailler

- Philippe Suchard

- Charles Kohler

- Roger Sprungli-Ammann

- Henri Nestle

- Rodolphe Lindt

- Jean Tobler

32. Read *The Chocolate Sundae Mystery (Boxcar Mystery #46)* by Gertrude Warner.

33. Research and create a list of Belgium chocolate pioneers.

34. Chocolatiers from Belgium use special techniques when creating their chocolate. Most confectioners receive their *couverteur* in heated tanker trucks soon after the *tempering* process. Because the chocolate has not had time to cool, the chocolate retains more of the aroma than the cooled varieties used by most producers.

- Find definitions for two chocolate terms: couverteur and tempering. Use your knowledge of these terms when learning how Belgium chocolates are made.

- Brainstorm reasons why this traditional Belgian process might make a better tasting chocolate.

35. Run over to your library and pick up the book entitled *Cocoa Ice* by Diana Applebaum.

36. Sort M&Ms by color. Make a graph displaying the number of M&Ms you have of each hue.

37. Check out *The Case of the Chocolate Fingerprints* by Parker C. Hinter.

38. Using a bag of M&Ms, discover the differences between mean, median, and mode. Have some fun as you discover the various types of averages together.

39. If you were Lizzie Lou, how would you rewrite the names for the recipes within this cookbook?

    • Need some help?

    • Names are more fun when they rhyme. Ex: Myrtle Turtle Cupcakes

40. Chocolate is considered an affordable luxury. Brainstorm a list of other affordable luxuries: $4.00 café latte vs. home-brewed cup of coffee, movie theater ticket vs. DVD rental, or video game vs. coloring book.

41. The French have a long history in the production of chocolate. Discover their specific contributions to the chocolate industry!

42. When you boil water, liquid changes into a gas.

When you bake a cake, the liquid batter transforms into a solid piece of cake. Amazing, isn't it? How does this happen? Delve into the subject of chemistry and find out why!

43. The ingredients in a recipe are generally written in two ways. Chefs either place the items in the order in which they are used or the chef will list the ingredients from the largest quantity to the smallest quantity. Place the ingredients used within the Chocolate Berry Cheesecake recipe (page 124) in order from the largest quantity to the smallest quantity. Here are a few tips to keep in mind:

    *1 gallon = 4 quarts

    *1 quart = 4 cups

    *1 pint = 2 cups

    *1 quart = 4 cups = 2 pints

    *1 tablespoon (T) = 3 teaspoons (t)

    * list single items (like eggs) last

When you see a fraction, think of it as a pizza pie. The largest piece is the larger fraction. Do not just look for the biggest numbers—that can easily trick you!

Chocolate Berry Cheesecake

INGREDIENTS:

2 cups chocolate cookie crumbs
1 gallon chocolate milk
1 quart hot fudge
1/4 cup butter, melted
5 cups cream cheese
2/3 cup sugar
1/2 cup sour cream
1 tablespoon grated orange peel
4 eggs
1/10 cup sour cream
2 tablespoons sugar
1 1/2 cups berries

44. Using another piece of paper, revise the instructions below using excellent grammar, spelling, and sentence construction.

Heat yer oven to 325 deegrees Mix them cookey crums and butter together in that there bowl. next, press the crumb mixtre onto the bottum and slightly up the side of a springform pan. Place the creemcheeze, sugar, sour cream and the ornge peel in yer food processor. Cover that whatchamacallit and prosess until that goop is smooth. Add them eggs next. Cover and prosess that mixture until smooth once agin. Be sure to spread all that there junk over the crust. bake about 1 hour and 20 minutes or until the center is set. Cool it on a wire rak for whatduyouthink...15 minutes. Run a medal spatula along side of chessecake to loosen; remove the side of that there pan. Gohead and stick her in the refrigerator uncovred for 3 howers; cover and continue refrigerating at least 4 additional howers. mix 1/10 cup sour cream and 2 T sugar in a bol. Spread it up on er cheesecake. top her off with them berries!

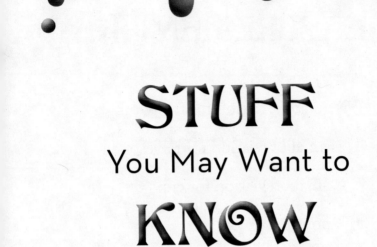

STUFF
You May Want to
KNOW

MEASUREMENT KEY

t. is an abbreviation for teaspoon

T. is an abbreviation for tablespoon

c. is an abbreviation for cup

lb = pound = 16 oz.

1 gallon = 4 quarts

1 quart = 4 cups

1 pint = 2 cups

1 quart = 4 cups = 2 pints

1 tablespoon = 3 teaspoons

GLOSSARY

Bake—To cook in a preheated oven.

Beat—To mix two or more ingredients with an electric mixer.

Blend—To mix two or more ingredients with a spoon until combined.

Boil—To heat a liquid in a saucepan until lots of bubbles rise and break on the surface. Steam also will begin to rise.

Chill—To place in the refrigerator until the item is cold.

Chop—To cut food into small pieces.

Crack an Egg—Tap the sides of an egg on the edge of a bowl to neatly crack the shell. Place the tips of both thumbs in the crack and open the shell, letting the egg yolk and white drop into the bowl.

Drizzle—Using the tip of the spoon to dribble steady lines of icing over your dessert.

Fold—To mix very gently.

Heat—To make something warm or hot by placing the saucepan on the stove burner that is turned on to the level it says within the recipe.

Measuring Dry Ingredients—Scoop up the dry ingredient to the top of the measuring cup or spoon. Use the back of a table knife to scrape off the excess so that the measure is perfectly level.

Measuring Liquid Ingredients—Place a clear glass measuring cup on a counter, finding the mark for the amount you need. Pour in the liquid up to that mark. Look at the mark at eye level to make sure the liquid meets the mark.

Melt—To heat a solid food (like chocolate or butter) until it turns into a liquid.

Scrape—To use a spatula to remove as much of a mixture as possible from inside a bowl.

Separating Egg Yolk from The White—

Two methods:

1. Place a wide-mesh strainer in a bowl. Carefully crack the egg into the strainer. Lift the strainer and let the white drip through the holes into a bowl. Pour the yolk into a different bowl.

2. Gently crack the egg in the middle, separating the shell into two halves. Place a bowl on a working surface directly under the egg. Pour the contents of the first egg half into the other half. The egg white will slide out into the bowl sitting below. Repeat this again until the yolk is the only part left in the eggshell.

Simmer—To heat liquids in a saucepan on low on the stove burner so that small bubbles appear on the surface.

Softened Butter—Butter that is at room temperature.

Spread—To cover the surface of something (for example: icing over cake).

Stir—To mix two or more ingredients with a spoon or rubber spatula, using a circular motion.

Visit the author online at

WWW.LIZZIELOUBOOKS.COM.